FIND OUT ABOUT

SPAIN

D1489328

WITHDRAWN
FROM THE RECORDS OF THE
MID-CONTINENT PUBLIC LIBRARY

J946 C883
Crosbie, Duncan.
Find out about spain

MID-CONTINENT PUBLIC LIBRARY
Blue Ridge Branch
9253 Blue Ridge Blvd.
Kansas City, MO 64138

BR

Where is Spain?

Europe is one of the five great continents of the world, and Spain is the third largest country in Europe. It occupies most of the square-shaped Iberian Peninsula and covers an area of 195,000 square miles.

This book will tell you all about Spain and its people. In Parts 1 and 2 you will go on a journey around the country to learn how people live and work, and how to pronounce Spanish words. In Part 3 there are lots of interesting facts about Spanish history, famous men and women, and places to see. Then in Part 4 you can learn some easy Spanish to use in different situations you might meet during your stay in one of Europe's largest and oldest countries.

You will meet the González family, and especially their son, Miguel, who is 11, and their daughter Carmen, who is 9. They will help you to learn some Spanish, and tell you about the things they enjoy doing.

Hi, I'm Miguel. You'll meet me again with my sister on page 13.

2

¿? Notice how the Spanish put an upside-down question mark in front of the sentence, and another – the "right" way up – at the end.

¡! They do the same with exclamation marks.

Talking to other people

There are two different words for "you" in Spanish. You use **tú** if you are speaking to people you know well, but **usted** (*oos-ted*) to someone you don't know very well.

Masculine and feminine words

In Spanish, all words are either masculine or feminine. **El banco** (*el ban-koh* – the bank) is masculine. **La leche** (*lah letch-eh* – milk) is feminine. If there is more than one, "the" becomes **los** (*loss*) if it is masculine, or **las** (*lass*) if it is feminine, for example, **los servicios** (*loss ser-vis-ios*) – toilets, **las patatas** (*lass pat-tat-as*) – potatoes.

Accents

á é í ó ú

Some vowels have an accent over them – a diagonal line that shows where the stress goes in the word. So **limón** (lemon) is said *lee-mohn*.

ñ There are 27 letters in the Spanish alphabet. The extra one is "n" with a squiggly line over it – **ñ**. You pronounce that *nya* – so **señor** (mister) is *seh-nyor*.

el banco
el ban-koh
bank

How to say Spanish words

j in Spanish is said like a soft *h*. The name Jaime is pronounced *Hi-meh,* for example. **Lejos** means "far" and you say *lay-hos.*

z is pronounced like a soft *th*. If you mention the big city of **Zaragoza**, you say *Thar-ar-goth-ah.* An apple is **manzana**, and you pronounce it *man-thah-nah.*

v is often pronounced like an English "b", so **verde**, meaning "green," is said *vehr-deh* or *behr-deh.*

e at the end of a word with two syllables or more is always pronounced as *eh*, so **grande** (big), for example, is *grahn-deh.*

qu is always spoken as *k*. So "cheese," which is **queso** in Spanish, is *keh-soh.* **Quince** (fifteen) is *kin-theh.*

ll is pronounced *yar* or *yeh* – **llame** (call) is said *yah-meh;* **llevar** (to carry) is *yeh-bahr.*

c is also pronounced with a soft *th* – provided it is followed by **e** or **i**. So if you see a sign in a shop window saying **cerrado** (closed) you say *ther-rah-doh.* If you want the station, you ask for **la estación**, *lah ess-tah-thee-ohn.*

But, when **c** is followed by **a**, **o,** or **u**, it is pronounced like a *k*. So **caliente**, meaning "hot" is spoken *kah-lee-en-teh.* "How much?" is **¿Cuánto?** and is pronounced *kwahn-toh.* This is confusing for non-Spanish speakers, but that's the way it is!

This may seem complicated, but you will soon get used to it. But there is something else to remember. This is how they say the words in Madrid and the north of Spain. In southern Spain and South America they do not follow these rules for **c**. There they pronounce it like **s**. In the big southern province of Andalucia you will hear them call it *An-dah-loo-see-ah.*

MID-CONTINENT PUBLIC LIBRARY

3 0000 12831189 5

MID-CONTINENT PUBLIC LIBRARY
Blue Ridge Branch
9253 Blue Ridge Blvd.
Kansas City, MO 64138
BR

Introduction

*Find out about what
Spanish people
do in their spare time.*

Did you know?

👍 Spain is the second-highest country in Europe. Its highest point is the Pico de Teide in Tenerife at 12,200 feet.

👍 There are 46,552 miles of railroad lines in Spain and it has the longest coastline in Europe.

👍 Spain has over 45 million visitors each year, making it the third most popular tourist destination in the world.

👍 The country was originally made up of several kingdoms and became united only in 1492.

👍 Spain is one of the oldest inhabited regions on the planet.

👍 Spain's fishing fleet is the largest in Europe. Fish forms an important part of the Spanish diet.

👍 There are more than 50 wine regions in Spain including Rioja, Navarra, and Rueda.

👍 Castillian is spoken by 74% of the population, Catalan by 17%, Galician by 7%, and Basque by 2%.

👍 The national anthem of Spain is called the *Marcha Real* (Royal March) and has no lyrics.

👍 There have been several attempts to compose lyrics for the *Marcha Real*, but they haven't been able to decide on one official version.

A journey around Spain

The capital of Spain is Madrid. The country has 17 different regions, each one very different from the others. They have their own customs, way of life, and food.

Travel around Spain is easy and there are plenty of places to stay. Despite the number of visitors to the country each year, it's possible to travel for days and hear only Spanish or one of the other three official languages being spoken.

The four official languages in Spain are Spanish itself, Catalan in the northeast, Basque in the north, and Galician in the north-west. The Catalan language is also spoken across the border in France (where it is called "Occitan") and the Basque language is also spoken in the region of France called Gascony.

Tapas

matador
ma-ta-dohr
bullfighter

recolector de naranjas
reh-koh-lehk-tohr deh nah-rang-kas
orange picker

mecánico
meh-kah-nee-koh
mechanic

bailaora
bye-lah-ora
flamenco dancer

5

Spain has a very good railroad system. It has high-speed trains called **Tren de Alta Velocidad**, or **AVE** for short, which run on special tracks. These connect all the main cities.

Spain had fewer highways than most European countries until recently. But now there are almost 5,000 miles of highways connecting major towns.

The coast of Spain is 4,900 miles long, and there is sea to the north, the east, and the south. Europeans from many other countries go there for a seaside vacation on one of the many beautiful beaches to enjoy swimming or windsurfing, and taste the wonderful seafood.

The Canaries

Balearic Islands

The seven Canary Islands, 700 miles away in the Atlantic Ocean, are part of Spain. So are Mallorca, Menorca, and Ibiza (called the Balearic Islands) in the Mediterranean Sea.

6

Because of its history, Spain can seem different from the rest of western Europe. In the eighth century southern and central Spain was conquered by the Moors, Moslem people from northern Africa. They ruled for 700 years before the country became Christian. There are many beautiful buildings from those times, such as the Alhambra and the Generalife in Granada, and the Great Mosque in Córdoba. The Moors' influence on buildings, gardens, and the use of water can still be seen. In surviving Moorish religious buildings, there are many geometric designs and patterns.

The Great Mosque, Córdoba

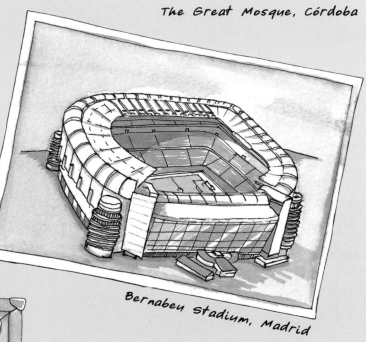

Bernabeu stadium, Madrid

Search **www.alhambra.org** for pictures of the beautiful Alhambra Palace.

Madrid and the big cities

Madrid (*mad-rid*) had fewer than 20,000 people when it was made the capital in 1561. But it grew quickly and has been the center of government ever since.

The Royal Palace

Although it does not have the long history that has made most other Spanish cities so interesting, it has some fine buildings and good museums.

Street sign in Madrid

The spectacular 400-year-old Plaza Mayor is full of cafés and restaurants and, like the rest of the city, is always bustling with life. No traffic is allowed there. The Fountain of Cibeles is also a good place to take photos and, if you are interested in painting, the Prado Museum has a magnificent collection of Old Masters.

Madrid may not be as picturesque as most Spanish cities, but its people live life to the fullest. You can even get stuck in a traffic jam at 4:00 in the morning!

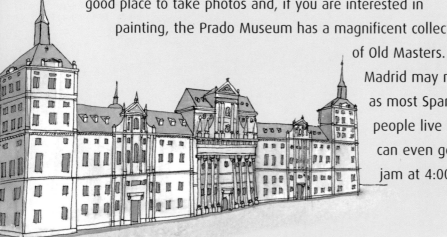

Visit **www.aboutmadrid.com** to find out more about the capital city.

Barcelona (*bar-seh-loh-nah*), on the northeast coast, is the proud capital of Catalonia. It is Spain's second biggest city and one of its major ports, and has always seen itself as important as Madrid. The Olympic Games were held in Barcelona in 1992. It has some of the most unusual buildings in Spain, many of them designed by the artist and architect, Gaudí.

Chimneys on the roof of the Casa Mila apartment block by Gaudí

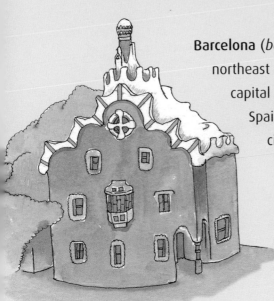

Antonio Gaudí's house in the Parc Guelle, Barcelona

La Giralda in Sevilla

Sevilla (*seh-vee-yah*) is the most important city in the great southern province of Andalucia. It was first established by the Moors as an inland harbor. It has magnificent buildings, some 800 years old and others brand new, like the ones made especially for the Universal Exhibition of 1992.

Tourist carriage, Sevilla

See if you can find out the name of the famous 18th-century bullring in Sevilla.

Valencia (*val-en-see-yah*) is the third largest city in Spain, and one of its most important ports. Valencia is a center of industry, and is best known for making beautifully designed and colorful tiles. The people of the city enjoy an energetic outdoor life, day and night.

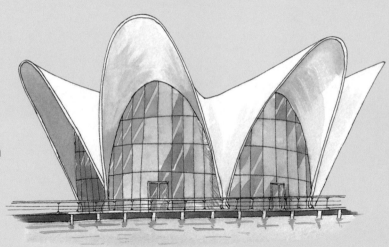

L'Oceanogràfic in Valencia's
City of Arts and Sciences

Bilbao (*bil-bow*) is the largest city in the Basque country in the north, and also Spain's busiest commercial port. It is an industrial city, with steelworks and chemical factories. In 1997 it opened the Guggenheim Museum in a highly original new building.

10 The Guggenheim Museum, Bilbao

 Use the Internet to find out the name of the festival held in Valencia every March.

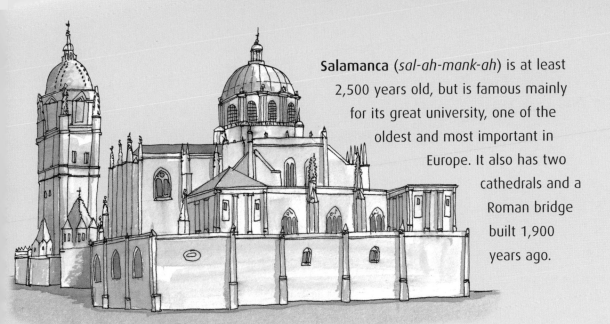

Salamanca (*sal-ah-mank-ah*) is at least 2,500 years old, but is famous mainly for its great university, one of the oldest and most important in Europe. It also has two cathedrals and a Roman bridge built 1,900 years ago.

One of the two cathedrals of Salamanca

Málaga (*mal-ah-gah*) is the second biggest city in Andalucia, after Sevilla. It has been a busy port for over 2,000 years, but today is also the center of the tourist industry on the south coast.

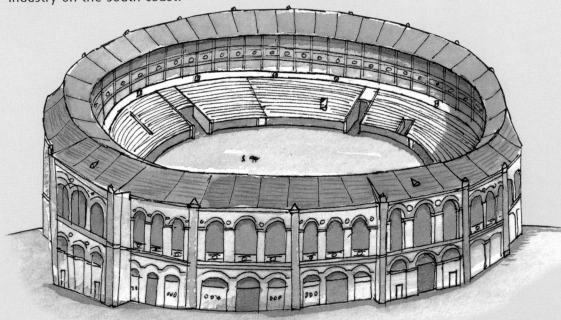

The bullring, Málaga

Visit www.aboutspain.net to find out more about big cities in Spain.

Sports

The Spanish are enthusiastic sportsmen and -women. Almost everyone loves to go cycling and many of them dream of winning a big competition like the Vuelta a España.

Soccer is immensely popular, and the leading clubs, Real Madrid and Barcelona, attract huge crowds, and stars such as David Beckham play for them.

All kinds of water sports are popular, and the Spanish are as excited about cycling as the French and Italians.

Bullfighting is almost a religion for the Spanish, especially in the south. For many, it represents tradition and an important way of life. The American author Ernest Hemingway was known for his passion for bullfighting.

Most of all, Spaniards just love life – especially eating and drinking outdoors with friends or family in the warm night air. Many still have a short sleep – a siesta – in the middle of the day, but at night they are rarely in bed before midnight!

Use your search engine to find the name of Spain's long-distance bicycle race.

Life in Spain

part two

Learn useful words and phrases that will help you when you visit Spain.

Did you know?

👍 Spanish people have 14 public holidays a year, which can be doubled if the holiday falls on a Tuesday or Thursday.

👍 The most important religious holiday in Spain is *Semana Santa*, the week before Easter, when people take part in large and lavish parades.

👍 The Spanish football league is called *La Liga* and is followed with passion by fans all over the world.

👍 All of Spain's regions are still dominated by their own cultures, traditions, and languages, making them all seem very different.

👍 The invasion of the Moors from North Africa contributed greatly to the Spanish way of life-its architecture, food, and agriculture.

👍 Shops in Spain close between 2 p.m. and 5 p.m. every day for the *siesta*, but department stores and supermarkets stay open until 9 p.m. or 10 p.m. without a break.

👍 Each region in Spain is very proud of its cuisine and many Spaniards believe their food is the best in the world.

👍 Lots of Spanish grownups still live with their parents, as traditionally, they don't leave home until they are married.

👍 The Spanish have one of the lowest birthrates of the world. Life is very busy!

Meet the family

Now you can start learning to speak some Spanish. Here is the González family (la familia González – *lah fam-ee-lyah Gon-thah-lez*) to help you get started. They will introduce you to different situations.

¡Bienvenida a España!
Byen-ben-ee-dah ah es-span-nya!
Welcome to Spain!

Nos llamamos Señor y Señora González.
Nos yah-mah-moss say-nyor ee say-nyor-rah gon-tha-lez.
We are called Mr. and Mrs. Gonzalez.

Me llamo Miguel.
Meh yah-moh mig-ehl.
My name is Miguel.

Y me llamo Carmen.
Ee meh yah-moh karr-men.
And my name is Carmen.

Miguel, Carmen, and their parents always speak in Spanish. Below the Spanish is a guide to help you pronounce it correctly, and the English is under that.

¡Bienvenida a España! – the Spanish words
byen-ben-ee-dah ah Es-span-nya! – how to say the Spanish words
Welcome to Spain! – what they mean in English

13

They will tell you about life in Spain – at home, at school, traveling, and having fun.

At school

Miguel and Carmen go to elementary school, which is called "la escuela primaria" (*lah ess-kway-lah pree-mar-ee-ah*). It is for children aged between 6 and 12 years old. School begins at 9 o'clock.

There are three hours of lessons in the morning, **la mañana** (*lah man-yah-nah*), and two hours in the afternoon, **la tarde** (*lah tar-deh*). Miguel and Carmen have one half-hour break in the playground in the morning, and one in the afternoon. Carmen is in the "second cycle," **segundo ciclo** (*ser-goon-doh thi-klo*) of her elementary school, so she has already begun learning a foreign language. English is the most popular foreign language, because it is useful all

el patio de recreo
ell pah-tyo deh ray-cray-yoh
playground

la pelota
lah peh-loh-tah
ball

el profesor
ell proh-fes-sor
teacher

la chica
lah chee-cah
girl

el chico
ell chee-coh
boy

over the world – but don't forget that almost as many people in the world speak Spanish or Chinese as use English! Miguel is in the "third cycle," **tercer ciclo** (*tair-thair thi-klo*), and he will leave elementary school at the end of the year, when he is 12.

La comida (*lah kom-ee-dah*) means lunch. All the children get an hour, and they go home if they live near enough. Miguel and Carmen live far away, so they bring a packed lunch with them.

Not many schools have sports or other activities outside the classroom. In some places, the parents organize clubs for activities like music, dance, drama, arts and crafts, and sports. Carmen is very interested in dance, and she does this twice a week with some of her school friends. Miguel is high on soccer and tennis, and there is a local sports club that runs classes for these after school.

la aula
lah owl-lah
classroom

la mochila
lah motch-ee-lah
schoolbag

el alumno
ell ah-loom-noh
student (boy)

la alumna
lah ah-loom-nah
student (girl)

el libro
ell lee-broh
book

el lápiz
ell lah-pees
pencil

la mesa
lah meh-sah
table

el cuaderno de ejercicios
ell quad-err-noh deh eh-hehr-sis-yos
exercise book

After school

Miguel and Carmen can't wait to get home once they have finished their schoolwork. There are so many things to do!

Sometimes they go around to play with their friends in their houses. Sometimes they watch cartoons on television. In Spanish these are called **los dibujos animados** (*loss dih-boo-hoss an-nim-ah-doss*).

After the cartoons, Miguel and Carmen might have a game together, or they might want to do their own things separately.

After a while, Miguel may get out his computer, called **el ordenador** (*ell or-den-ah-dohr*) or, in South America, **la computadora** (*lah kom-poo-tah-doh-rah*). Sometimes he plays computer games or he may go on the Internet, **el internet**, to find out things he needs for school. While Carmen waits for her turn at the computer, she reads a popular comic book about Mortadelo y Filemón.

The Spanish like to eat well, and Señora González takes great care to buy fresh food. She goes to the local market at least twice a week to find fresh meat, fish, vegetables, cheese, and fruit. In Spain, people have dinner very late, especially in the south where the climate is so hot. The whole family has dinner – **la cena** (*lah thay-nah*) together. Eating in front of the television is definitely not allowed!

After dinner, it's time for Carmen to have her bath and go to bed. Miguel is allowed to stay up later, so he starts to read Carmen's comic books!

el ordenador
ell or-den-ah-dohr
computer

16

Why not visit **www.mortadeloyfilemon.com** to see the sort of comics Spanish kids read.

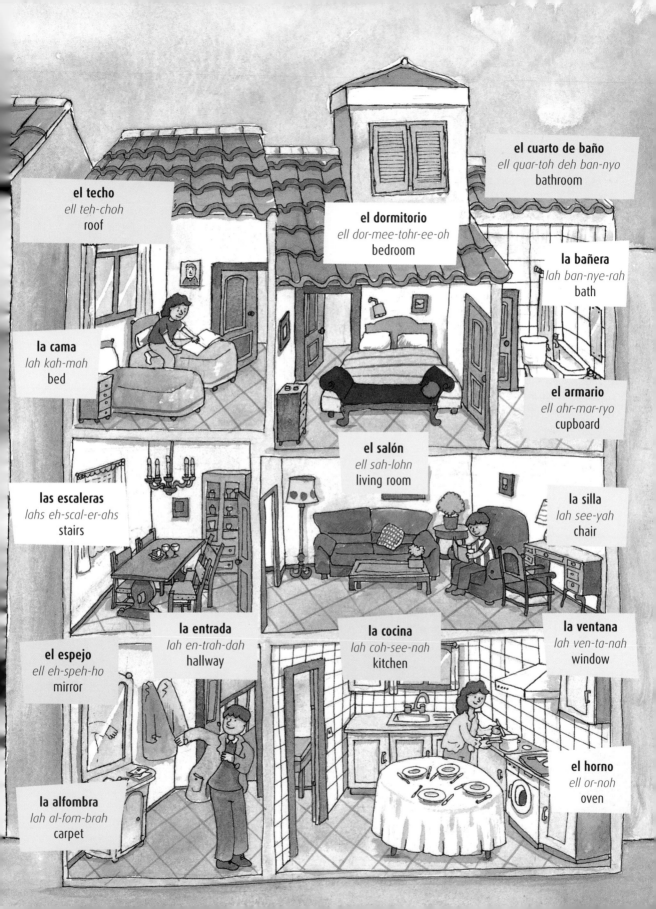

el cuarto de baño
ell quar-toh deh ban-nyo
bathroom

el techo
ell teh-choh
roof

el dormitorio
ell dor-mee-tohr-ee-oh
bedroom

la bañera
lah ban-nye-rah
bath

la cama
lah kah-mah
bed

el armario
ell ahr-mar-ryo
cupboard

el salón
ell sah-lohn
living room

las escaleras
lahs eh-scal-er-ahs
stairs

la silla
lah see-yah
chair

la entrada
lah en-trah-dah
hallway

la cocina
lah coh-see-nah
kitchen

la ventana
lah ven-ta-nah
window

el espejo
ell eh-speh-ho
mirror

el horno
ell or-noh
oven

la alfombra
lah al-fom-brah
carpet

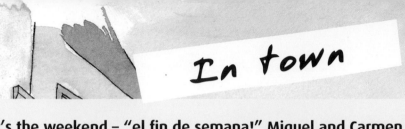

In town

It's the weekend – "el fin de semana!" Miguel and Carmen love the weekend because there's no school and they can play as much as they like. Señor and Señora González like it too, because they don't have to go to work.

el ayuntamiento
ell ah-yoon-tah-mee-en-toh
the town hall

la iglesia
lah ig-lay-see-ah
the church

el quiosco de periódicos
ell key-oss-koh deh pair-ee-od-dik-oss
the stationery and newspaper shop

el correos
ell kohr-reh-oss
the post office

el banco
ell ban-koh
the bank

la pastelería
lah pass-tel-er-ree-ah
the pastry shop

la farmacia
lah far-mah-thee-ah
the pharmacy

el supermercado
ell soo-pehr-mer-kah-doh
the supermarket

la gasolinera
lah gas-oh-lee-neh-rah
the gas station

la tienda de comestibles
*lah tee-en-dah deh
koh-mes-tee-bless*
the grocery store

While Sra. González is at the market, Miguel goes to the park to play football with his friends. In the afternoon, he goes in the car with his father to get gas at the gas station in town.

Things people do

Spain is a large country bordered by the Atlantic and the Mediterranean, with many mountains and high plateaus. There are many variations in the climate – mostly hot in summer, in winter often very wet or very cold.

Spain is a very important farming country, and sells food all over Europe.

In the dry areas of Spain, olives, grapes, and wheat are grown. Spain is the biggest producer of olive oil in Europe. It also has the most vineyards in the world, but is only the third biggest winemaker.

las aceitunas
lass ah-say-too-nahs
olives

el pastor
ell pas-tor
sheepherder

Sheep farming is common on the high plains of central Spain, and this is where much of Spain's cheese is produced.

Spain produces many good wines, but it is famous for a strong wine made in the south called sherry. This has been a popular drink in many countries for hundreds of years.

la oveja
lah oh-veh-ha
sheep

el vino de jerez
ell bee-noh deh heh-rezz
sherry

20

Lemons and oranges are grown all along the south and east coasts of Spain and exported all over the world. Spain is also famous for its almond trees (**las almendras** – *lass almen-drahs*). They grow on dry hillsides, and the nuts are used in cooking and drink making. Because of the high rainfall, there is dairy farming in the green, rolling fields of the north.

The north coast is also the center of the Spanish fishing industry, which is very strong. Only the Portuguese eat more seafood than the Spanish.

las naranjas
lass nah-rahn-has
oranges

el pescador
ell pes-kah-dor
fisherman

el barco pesquero
ell bahr-koh pess-squeh-roh
fishing boat

21

What's made in Spain? Type "Spain" and an industry in your search engine to find out.

Because they produce so much food of many different kinds, the Spanish enjoy eating well. The Spanish often eat in restaurants rather than at home. Partly for this reason, many people work in hotels, cafés, and restaurants. This is also because tourism is so important to Spain. Millions of people come each year to enjoy sand and sea, to explore the ancient towns and villages inland, and to hike in the hills and mountains.

Spain also builds ships and cars, and is an important country for manufacturing cloth and making clothes.

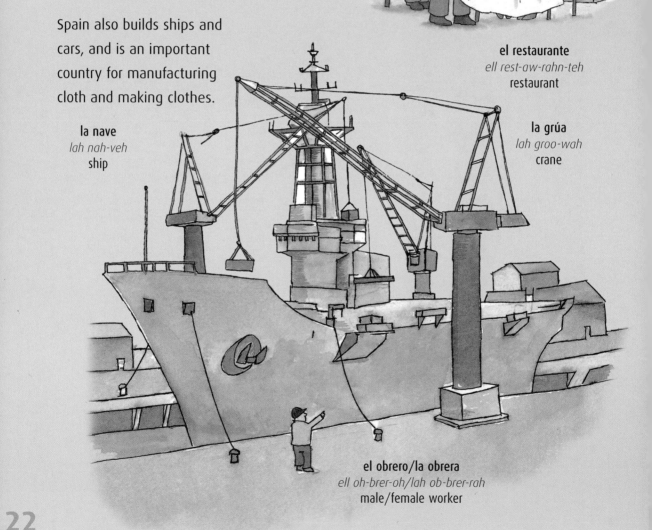

el restaurante
ell rest-aw-rahn-teh
restaurant

la grúa
lah groo-wah
crane

la nave
lah nah-veh
ship

el obrero/la obrera
ell oh-brer-oh/lah ob-brer-rah
male/female worker

22

Have a look on the Internet to find out more about Spanish food.

Things about Spain

part three

Did you know?

👍 Saint James, who is said to be buried in Compostela in the north, is Spain's patron Saint.

👍 Goya's paintings and engravings have been some of the most influential works of art for contemporary artists.

👍 The Hollywood actors Antonio Banderas and Penelope Cruz started off as stars in films by Spain's favorite director, Pedro Almodóvar.

👍 There are more restaurants, cafes, and bars in Spain than in any other country in the world.

👍 In Valencia, in August, 30,000 people gather together to take part in a massive food fight with more than 24,000 pounds of tomatoes to celebrate the harvest.

👍 On the hilltops in Spain you will see large cut-outs of bulls, which are left over from an advertising campaign in the 1980s. They have since become a symbol of Spain.

👍 The bulls used in bullfighting have to be a specific breed called the *Toro Bravo*, which exists only in Spain.

👍 Galicia, in the northeast, is renowned for having the best ingredients and tastiest recipes in Spain.

👍 Over one million people, including tourists and Spaniards, go to watch bullfights every year. Good matadors are famous all over the country.

50 Spanish history facts

1 Between 18,000 and 14,000 B.C. Cave paintings were made by prehistoric people at Altamira, Ribasdella, and Nerja.

2 1200 B.C. The Talaiotic people of Menorca build hundreds of stone villages and buildings of three different types.

Talaiotic building remains

3 218 B.C. The Romans invade Spain, and complete their settlement of the country by **74 A.D**.

4 711–785 The Moors settle in southern Spain and rule there for seven hundred years.

5 778 The Basques defeat part of Charlemagne's army led by Roland at the Battle of Roncesvalles. An epic poem called *The Song of Roland* is written.

6 785 The building of the Great Mosque (the Mezquita) is begun in Córdoba. It is one of the world's finest buildings.

The Mezquita in Córdoba

7 1094 El Cid captures Valencia from the Moors. He and his wife Jimena are buried in Burgos Cathedral.

8 1143 Portugal separates from the Spanish kingdoms, and becomes a monarchy in its own right.

9 1180 The epic poem *El Cantar del Mío Cid*, immortalizing El Cid, is written.

El Cid

10 1238 The Nasrid dynasty takes power in Granada, and the building of the Alhambra begins.

Cave painting at Altamira

23

Find out about Roland at www.AllRefer.com – look in the encyclopedia, under R.

11 **1480** The Spanish Inquisition is set up and becomes one of the cruelest and bloodiest systems of religious persecution. It lasts until the 18th century.

12 **1492** The Catholic monarchs, Ferdinand and Isabella, drive the Moors from Granada and unite most of Spain under Christian rule.

Ferdinand and Isabella

13 **1492** Columbus discovers the Americas.

14 **1512** The Kingdom of Navarre is added to Spain, and it becomes the united country we know today.

15 **1519** Cortes invades Mexico and makes it part of the Spanish Empire.

16 **1580–1640** Portugal unites with Spain for a sixty-year period.

17 **1588** Naval Armada is sent against England, fails, and is broken up.

18 **1605** One of the greatest works in Spanish literature, *Don Quijote* by Cervantes, is published.

Don Quijote

19 **1746** Francisco Goya, probably the best known of all Spain's great painters, is born.

20 **1805** Combined French and Spanish fleet is routed by Nelson at the Battle of Trafalgar, off Cádiz.

21 **1808** The people of Madrid rebel against Napoleon's occupying troops, and are brutally crushed. This starts the War of Independence, 1808–14.

22 **1809** Spanish troops join the British under the Duke of Wellington to beat the French at the Battle of Talavera.

23 **1881** Pablo Picasso, one of the greatest of 20th-century painters, is born in Málaga.

24 **1888** The Universal Exhibition is held in Barcelona, and the revolutionary Modernista school of architecture is born.

Which day is celebrated on the 2nd Monday of October every year in the United States?

25 **1895** The Cuban War of Independence is a disaster for Spain, which loses 50,000 soldiers and most of its navy.

"Tragic Week" in Barcelona

26 **1898** Cuba and the Philippines become independent from Spain.

27 **1909** "Tragic Week" in Barcelona, when workers take to the streets to protest against military conscription, and are shot down by government troops.

28 **1923** Primo de Rivera seizes power in a coup d'état, and rules as dictator for seven years.

29 **1929** Universal Exhibitions in Barcelona and Sevilla bring international recognition, and stimulate new art forms.

30 **1936** The Nationalists under General Franco rebel against the Republicans after the latter win the General Election. Brutal civil war from 1936–39.

General Franco

31 **1936** The poet and playwright Federico Garcia Lorca is executed by a Nationalist firing squad.

32 **1937** Nazi Germany sides with Franco, and bombs defenseless Guernica, inspiring one of Picasso's most celebrated paintings in protest.

Attack on Guernica

33 **1939** The Fascist General Franco becomes dictator. Spain is politically isolated from 1945 until it joins the United Nations in 1955.

34 **1956** Soccer's European Cup for clubs is inaugurated, and the great Real Madrid team win it five successive times – 1956–60.

35 **1962** Tourism from abroad is stimulated, and quickly grows into a major industry.

The tourist industry

36 **1973** The Spanish coast is transformed as sun-seeking foreign tourists grow to 34 million a year.

37 **1975** Franco dies, and the monarchy is restored under King Juan Carlos, grandson of the king before Franco, Alfonso XIII.

King Juan Carlos

What nationality is Queen Sofia, wife of King Juan Carlos? ☞

38 **1977** The first free elections since 1936 are held.

39 **1981** Spain's Civil Guard attempts a coup d'état, holding the government at gunpoint. The king demands their surrender, and the coup fails.

Civil Guard rebel leader

40 **1982** Soccer's prestigious World Cup is held in Spain, but the home country fails to get beyond the second stage. Italy beats West Germany in the final.

The Jules Rimet Trophy

41 **1982** Spain's Socialist party under Felipe González wins a landslide victory and introduces major changes.

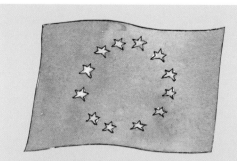

42 **1986** Spain joins the European Union and begins a period of rapid economic growth.

43 **1992** The Universal Exhibition is again held in Sevilla, with over a hundred countries taking part. Many exciting new buildings are designed for it.

44 **1992** The Olympic Games are held in Barcelona and are an outstanding success.

45 **1995** Miguel Indurain wins the world-famous Tour de France for the fifth time, a feat never before achieved.

46 **1997** The astonishing Guggenheim Museum is opened in Bilbao, symbolizing the regrowth of Spanish culture after Franco's fascism.

47 **2002** Real Madrid wins soccer's European Cup – a record ninth time.

48 **2002** Spain joins most other countries of the European Union in replacing its old currency with the euro.

One euro

49 **2004** On March 11, terrorist bombs on commuter trains kill over a hundred people in Madrid's Atocha station.

50 **2007** Spain's high-speed rail service, the AVE, begun in 1992 from Madrid to Sevilla, is due to be completed countrywide.

At **www.realmadrid.com**, click Track Record to find when Real Madrid won the European Cup.

Famous people

Rulers

Ferdinand of Aragón and **Isabella of Castille** (15th cent) united Spain when they married in 1469, and drove the Moors from Granada, their last stronghold in 1492.

Carlos I (1500–58) ruled Spain and was also king of the Netherlands, king of Sicily and the Holy Roman Emperor (1519–58). Under him, Spanish power was at its greatest.

Carlos I

Felipe (Philip) II (1527–98) married Queen Mary of England in 1554, and sent the Armada to destruction against Queen Elizabeth of England in 1588.

Primo de Rivera (1870–1930) carried out a coup d'état in 1923 and established a military dictatorship from 1923–30.

Francisco Franco (1892–1975) began the brutal Spanish Civil War in 1936, and became dictator from 1939 until his death. He held back Spanish development for a generation.

Juan Carlos I (b. 1939) The monarchy was restored after Franco's death in 1975. Juan Carlos won admiration for reintroducing democracy. Thanks to him an attempted coup d'état in 1981 failed.

Felipe González (b. 1942) Spain's first Socialist prime minister was elected in 1982, and during the next 13 years helped transform Spain into a thoroughly modern country.

Soldiers and explorers

El Cid (Rodrigo Díaz de Vivar, 1043-99) Heroic figure who fought (on both sides) in the 11th-century Christian-Moorish wars.

Cristóbal Colón (Christopher Columbus, 1451–1506) Italian-born sailor who was sent by Ferdinand and Isabella to find the East Indies, but discovered Central America instead.

Francisco Pizarro (1475–1541) invaded Peru in 1532, captured and executed the Inca ruler Atahualpa. He was eventually murdered by his own followers.

Francisco Pizarro

27

Find out about Felipe González. How many general elections did he win?

Cortés

Hernán Cortés

(1484–1547) invaded Mexico in 1519. He defeated the Aztecs under Montezuma, and made Mexico a Spanish province.

Admiral Federico Gravina (1756–1806) Brilliant sailor, first appointed Spanish Ambassador to France and later Commander-in-Chief of the Spanish navy.

Sportsmen and -women

Pedro Romero (1755–1845) Known as the father of modern bullfighting, who killed over 6,000 bulls in his career. He retired without a scratch on him at the age of 72.

"El Cordobés" (Manuel Benítez – b. 1936) Probably the most famous of recent bullfighters, he became a national idol in the 1960s for his acrobatic and unorthodox style.

Ricardo Zamora (1901–78) Successful soccer goalkeeper for many years who played 46 times for his country. He was the hero of his country's first win against England in 1929.

Luis Suárez (b. 1935) Played 32 times for Spain at soccer. Helped Spain win the European Champions Cup in 1964; played in the World Cup in 1962 and 1966.

Manuel Santana

(b. 1938) Spain's greatest tennis player, who won Wimbledon in 1966, the French Open in 1961 and 1964, and the U.S. Open (on grass) in 1965.

Manuel Santana

Seve Ballesteros

(b. 1957) A thrilling golfer who won five major tournaments. In 2000 he was named European Golfer of the Century, and Spanish Sportsman of the Century.

Arantxa Sánchez Vicario (b. 1971) Tennis player who won the French Open in 1989, 1994, and 1998, and the U.S. Open in 1994.

Conchita Martínez

(b. 1972) Tennis player who won acclaim for her grass court victory at Wimbledon in 1994.

José Antonio Reyes (b. 1983) Outstanding Spanish soccer player who joined the English club Arsenal for a record $30 million in 2004.

El Cordobés

28

Writers and philosophers

Miguel de Cervantes (1547–1616) One of Spain's greatest writers, best known for his novel *Don Quijote*, published in 1605.

Félix Lope de Vega (1562–1635) The great playwright of Spain's "Golden Age" in the 16th and 17th centuries. He wrote over 2,000 plays, of which 500 survive today.

Federico García Lorca (1898–1936) Poet and dramatist, who was shot in the Spanish Civil War. His best-known play is *La Casa de Bernarda Alba* (*The House of Bernarda Alba*).

Federico Garcia Lorca

Painters and musicians

El Greco (1544–1614) Greek by birth, El Greco lived the second half of his life in Toledo, and painted his best works there.

Velázquez (1599–1660) Famous for two kinds of paintings – of the royal court, and of ordinary Spanish family life.

Francisco de Goya (1746–1828) Probably the greatest of all Spanish painters; his work drew attention to the injustice and the cruelty of war.

Pablo Picasso (1881–1973) One of the most famous 20th-century painters; he lived mainly in France. *Guernica* (1937), an angry protest against war, is his best-known work.

Salvador Dalí

Salvador Dalí (1904–89) eccentric Surrealist artist who used images from his dreams to create bizarre, yet beautiful paintings.

Pablo Casals (1876–1973) Composer, conductor, and cellist, Casals was Spain's most world-famous musician. Lived in exile after 1936, dying just before Spain was freed from fascism.

Manuel de Falla (1876–1946) Spain's greatest 20th-century composer, whose best-known work is *Nights in the Gardens of Spain*. Left Spain for Argentina, in 1939 after the Civil War.

Andrés Segovia (1894–1987) Guitarist who succeeded by his technique in showing that the guitar is suitable for playing classical music. Composers then began to write for it.

Andrés Segovia

Joaquín Rodrigo (1901–99) Noted 20th-century composer, his best-known work is the *Concierto de Aranjuez* for the guitar.

29

Have a look at some of Dalí's most famous paintings at www.virtualdali.com

Singers, film stars, and directors

Victoria de los Ángeles (b. 1923), **Montserrat Caballé** (b. 1933), **Plácido Domingo** (b. 1944), and **José Carreras** (b. 1946) are

Victoria de los Angeles

four of the great international superstars of opera. Two of them, de los Ángeles and Carreras, are Catalans from Barcelona.

Ana Belén (b. 1951) Talented international singer and actress who, in the 1980s, was voted the most admired woman in Spain.

Julio Iglesias (b. 1943) The most popular crooner in Spain – indeed the world. He has sold 160 million albums, more than any other singer in history.

Camarón de la Isla (1952–92) Music and song is as important as dance in flamenco, and this gypsy from Cádiz was the most famous modern singer.

Enrique Iglesias (b. 1975) Son of Julio, singer and songwriter; his first Spanish album sold half a million in its first week.

Antonio Ruiz Soler (1922–96) One of the greatest of Andalusia's flamenco dancers.

Luis Buñuel (1900–83) One of the world's great film directors; he made seven outstanding masterpieces late in life, probably the best-remembered being *Belle de Jour* (1967).

Pedro Almodóvar (b. 1949) Spain's best-known modern film director. In 2000 his film *Todo sobre mi madre* (*All About My Mother*) won an Oscar for Best Foreign Film.

Architects

Antoni Gaudí

Antoni Gaudí (1852–1926) Together with **Josep Puig** and **Lluís Domenech**, Gaudí was the most original and noted architect responsible for the Modernista movement in Barcelona.

Fashion

The end of the Franco dictatorship released much creative talent in Spanish fashion design. Names that have become famous worldwide in the last thirty years include **Pedro del Hierro**, **Paco Rabanne**, **Agatha Ruiz de la Prada**, **Antonio Miró**, **Nacho Ruiz**, and **Roberto Verino**.

Paco Rabanne

 Find Julio Iglesias' 1968 competition-winning song at **www.julioiglesias.com**

Things to see

The Prado Museum

Madrid

Plaza Mayor The large and beautiful square that is the beating heart of the old city, with many bars, restaurants, and shops.

Prado Museum The Royal collection is the greatest display of Spanish painting anywhere in the world.

Museo del Aire, Carretera de Extremadura, 7 miles from Madrid. The museum displays many fascinating old planes, including the Breguet XIX that flew the Atlantic in 1929.

Barcelona

Sagrada Familia Gaudí's unique cathedral was started in 1882 and is still being built. Original and unforgettable.

Casa Mila (also known as La Pedrera) Another extraordinary building by Gaudí. One of many exciting buildings in the "Golden Square" of Barcelona.

Poble Espanyol The Spanish Village was created for the Universal Exhibition of 1929 to display the different architecture of the country's regions. It was restored in the 1980s.

Parque Güell An astonishing and colorful creation by Gaudí, this World Heritage site is a garden city spread over 50 acres. It dates mainly from 1910–14.

Northeast

Teatro-Museo Dalí, Figueres This unique museum was planned by the surrealist painter, Salvador Dalí. After the Prado, it is Spain's most visited museum.

Teatro-Museo Dalí, Figueres

31

Can you find out what "The Big Three" in Madrid are?

North and northwest

Santiago de Compostela

Santiago de Compostela The most important place of medieval pilgrimage after Jerusalem and Rome. Still attracts thousands of visitors every year.

Guggenheim Museum, Bilbao American architect Frank Gehry's amazing building, opened in 1997.

Puente la Reina A beautiful, five-arched bridge was built nearly one thousand years ago for pilgrims going to Santiago.

Pamplona The most famous sight is the annual running of the bulls at 8 o'clock every morning from July 6–14.

Cuenca The picturesque old town is built on a cliff between the gorges of two rivers, with houses hanging out over the sheer drops.

Torre de Hércules, A Coruña Europe's oldest working lighthouse.

Central Spain

Toledo Historic city, and the home of the El Greco Museum that contains many of this great painter's works – including views of the city 400 years ago.

Segovia The 1st-century Roman aqueduct was used for 1,800 years. A fairy-tale *Alcázar* (castle) rises above the city. There is a magnificent cathedral.

Ávila The most complete medieval walls anywhere in Europe, over a mile long with 88 towers.

Windmills of La Mancha On a ridge above Consuegra there are eleven white windmills with thatched roofs, like the ones in Cervantes' famous book *Don Quijote*.

Caves of Valporquero These great limestone caves beneath the village of Valporquero stretch for 10,000 feet, and are between 5 and 25 million years old.

The walls of Ávila

What unusual material did Frank Gehry use in building the Guggenheim Museum, Bilbao?

The West

Cáceres A beautiful Renaissance town from the 15th century, with stately old homes and watchtowers, Cáceres was the first place in Spain to be named a "heritage city."

Guadalupe Monastery The 14th-century monastery has romantic towers and turrets. Its most famous treasure is the Black Virgin – black from candle smoke.

The South

Mérida Site of one of the best-preserved Roman theaters in the world.

Sevilla: La Giralda The bell tower of the great cathedral. You can climb to the top for a fine view of the city.

Sevilla: Real Alcázar The royal palace, begun in 1364, contains some of the finest Moorish craftsmanship.

The Roman theater at Mérida

The Alhambra, Granada

Córdoba: The Mezquita Begun by Abd al Rahman in 785, this World Heritage site is so large that the 16th-century cathedral built in the middle of it is barely noticeable.

Granada: The Alhambra Built by the Moorish kings in the 13th and 14th centuries, it is a magical mix of buildings, courtyards, arcades, and water.

Granada: The Generalife Above the Alhambra are the 13th-century gardens and summer palace of the Moorish kings.

Garganta del Chorro Not far from Málaga is a gorge cut through the mountain by the Chorro river. It is 590 feet deep but (in places) only 30 feet wide.

Málaga: The Alcazaba A castle built 1,300 years ago on the site of a Roman fortress.

Málaga: Nature Reserve de los Montes In the hills to the north of Málaga, eagles and wild boar still thrive. There are well-marked paths among the lavender and wild flowers.

Plaza de Toros, Ronda

Ronda: Plaza de Toros Bullring opened in 1785 and often called "the spiritual home of bullfighting."

Ronda: Puente Nuevo Impressive 300-foot bridge built across the gorge of the river Tagus in the 18th century.

Coto de Doñana National Park North of Cádiz is one of Europe's greatest wetlands. Visitors are taken in on small, high-wheeled buses to prevent damage to the environment.

The Balearic islands

Mallorca: Palma Cathedral Dazzling white 16th-century cathedral looks like a great ship floating on the blue sea.

Mallorca: The railway to Sóller A narrow-gauge line with small wooden carriages goes from Palma to the mountain town of Sóller.

Mallorca: The Del Drac Caves Contain four huge chambers – Diana's Bath, the Enchanted City, and Theater of the Fairies are three of them.

Menorca Called an "immense open-air museum" because there are hundreds of stone buildings and ruins, between 3,000 and 4,000 years old, covering the island.

The Canary Islands

Lanzarote: Mountains of Fire Active volcanos. You can ride camels up the mountain slopes and tour the lunar landscape.

Tenerife: the Dragon trees Known to be hundreds of years old.

Tenerife: Mt. Teide National Park – The land around Spain's highest mountain is wild, with *cañadas* – gravelly "lakes" –and weirdly shaped rocks. *Planet of the Apes* was filmed here.

Dragon tree

 What is the name of the famous caves in the east of the island of Mallorca?

50 facts about Spain

Mount Teide

1 Spain is 194,898 square miles in size, including the Canary and Balearic islands.

2 The mainland is 500 miles from north to south, and 550 from east to west.

3 For 600 years, Spain has also owned two tiny islands off the Moroccan coast – Ceuta and Melilla.

4 Britain owns the Rock of Gibraltar at the entrance to the Mediterranean.

5 Spain is the second-highest country in Europe with an average altitude of 2,132 feet above sea level.

Gibraltar

6 Madrid is the highest capital city in Europe.

7 At 12,198 feet, Mt. Teide on the island of Tenerife is Spain's highest mountain.

8 Spain's main river is the Ebro, and it is the only river to flow south into the Mediterranean.

9 Half of Spain's soil is unproductive, and inland from Almeria, in the southeast, it is almost desert.

10 Spain is the ninth-wealthiest country in the world.

11 The Spanish currency is the euro. There are 100 cents in one euro and the sign is €.

12 Only one in every ten Spaniards buys a daily newspaper.

13 Spain's best-selling newspaper, *El País*, was started only in 1976.

El País

35

At **www.spain-info.com** , find out where the film *Lawrence of Arabia* was made.

14 Spain's famous drink, sherry, comes from Jerez de la Frontera in the south. The name sherry comes from English efforts to pronounce *Jerez*.

15 Spain has more acres of vineyards (about 20 million) than any country in the world.

16 Spain has over 300 varieties of cheese, but eats less cheese than any other European country.

Sheep's milk cheese

17 Spain has nearly 4,900 miles of coastline, so it's not surprising that every kind of water sport can be enjoyed there.

18 Fuerteventura in the Canary Islands claims to have the best windsurfing in the world – competing with the Cape Verde islands to the south.

Windsurfing

19 Tarifa, on Spain's southeast coast, is the windiest place in Europe – so the windsurfing is pretty good there too.

20 Spain has 1,240 miles of beaches (*playas*), mostly on the east and south coasts, and in the Canary and Balearic islands.

21 Spain has over 30 ski resorts located in 14 provinces.

22 Spain hosted the World Cup Skiing championships in 1996. (It should have been 1995 but was postponed due to lack of snow.)

Skiing

23 Although the Spanish are not avid hikers, there are tens of thousands of miles of official footpaths. Many foreigners come to walk on them.

24 The most famous of all footpaths is the old Pilgrim's Way through the Pyrenees to Santiago de Compostela in northwest Spain.

25 The Coto de Doñana, near Cádiz, is Europe's largest nature reserve.

36

At **www.jrnet.com/travel** find out about the Pilgrims' Way (*Camino de Santiago*).

26 There are 12 national parks and over 200 nature reserves in Spain.

27 Although the Spanish are crazy about soccer, Spain has never won the World Cup. It did win the European soccer championship in 1964.

28 Spain's two biggest soccer clubs are Real Madrid, whose Bernabeu Stadium holds 130,000, and Barcelona, whose Nou Camp stadium holds 120,000.

29 No one had ever won the *Tour de France* 5 times running before Spain's Miguel Indurain 1991–95. (Since then, Lance Armstrong has won it 7 times.)

30 The *Vuelta a España* is the world's third most important cycle race, after the Tours of France and Italy. It lasts three weeks.

31 Every July during the Los Samfermines fiesta in Pamplona, six bulls are released daily in the streets at 8 a.m. and young men run before them.

The Bull Run in Pamplona

32 There are more than 8,000 bars and pubs in Madrid – that's one for every 600 inhabitants!

Tickets for *El Gordo*

33 Every Christmas, Spain runs the world's biggest lottery, called *El Gordo* (The Fat One). Ticket sales are about $1.7 billion.

34 One of the world's leading art galleries is the *Prado* in Madrid. It has over 5,000 masterpieces.

35 In 1950, only 37% of the population lived in towns of more than 10,000. By 2000, that figure had grown to 65%.

36 The average summer temperature in the western region of Extremadura is 106°F (41°C). That makes it a very hot place indeed!

37 Average winter rainfall in the northern Basque country is 4¾ inches, yet in the region next to it, Aragón, it is only ¾ inch.

38 Tourism accounts for about 10% of Spain's annual earnings.

Carmen

39 The Spanish eat more seafood per head than any other European nation except Portugal.

40 The San Sebastian Film Festival is one of the five leading film festivals in Europe.

41 In the northwest region of Galicia they speak *Gallego*, a language a little bit like Portuguese.

42 In Galicia bagpipes are the favorite musical instrument.

43 A feature of many annual fiestas in Catalonia is the *castellars* – men who build human towers that can be up to seven people high.

44 In the Basque game of *pelota*, in which a ball is hit against three walls at right angles, the ball can reach speeds of over 120 mph.

45 The Madrid metro is Spain's oldest subway system. It has 12 lines, 160 stations, and carries 565 million passengers a year.

46 Madrid taxi drivers are among the most polite in the world – but few of them will take dogs in their cabs!

47 The old Kingdom of Castille (now the region of Castilla y León) got its name from the hundreds of castles built during the wars of the 11th century.

48 In the famous opera *Carmen*, the heroine works in a Sevilla tobacco factory. The factory is still there, and is now part of the Universidad de Sevilla.

49 In the 1960s and 1970s, spaghetti westerns, including *The Good, the Bad, and the Ugly* and *A Fistful of Dollars* were made in the desert around Tabernas in the south.

50 The prehistoric remains on the Balearic island of Menorca are among the richest in the world with hundreds of 3,000–4,000 year-old buildings.

Castellars

When was Georges Bizet's opera Carmen first performed? Search www.r-ds.com/opera

Let's learn Spanish

Join Miguel and Carmen on vacation in Barcelona and learn all about the beautiful city.

part four

Did you know?

👍 Euskara, the language spoken in the Basque region of Spain, is one of the oldest living languages in the world.

👍 Lunchtime is very important to the Spanish and most people go home from work every day to eat with their families.

👍 Family time is very important, and you will often see several generations of relatives gathering to enjoy eating together.

👍 When you buy a drink in Spain, you will also be given a small snack called a *tapa*; it can be anything from a few olives to a piece of *tortilla* or a mini-burger.

👍 The word *tapas* comes from the plate that was used by Spaniards to protect their drinks from flies. Translated, *tapa* literally means cap or lid.

👍 *Paella* is a typically Spanish dish made of rice, fish, meat, and vegetables that are all cooked together in a huge frying pan.

👍 Some of the best ham in the world comes from the Extremadura area of Spain and is called *jamón serran*

👍 Whole legs of ham are stored on hooks hanging from ceilings in bars and restaurants to mature the flavor of the meat.

👍 The art of bullfighting is celebrated in Spain as a national treasure and is called *La Tauromaq*

Speaking Spanish

When you arrive and hear Spanish people speaking fast, you may feel a bit frightened, but it's easier than you think to get started.

Like people everywhere, the Spanish are pleased when you make the effort to speak a few words of their language – just as you would be if someone speaking a foreign language came to your town and had already learned a few words of English. When they see you are trying, they will often smile and try to help you in return – especially outside Madrid where they don't see so many foreigners.

por favor
pohr fah-bohr
please

Hi! In the next few pages Carmen and I will show you some useful words for your vacation in Spain.

gracias
grar-thee-as
thank you

buenas noches
bweh-nahs noh-chez
good night

Start with a few simple words like "hello" or "good morning" and "good night." Always remember to say "please" and "thank you."

Then you can try **¿está bien?** *(es-tah bee-en?)* with a rising voice to ask "Is that OK?" when you hand over some money for a postcard or some candy. If you want something in a shop you can point at it and say **¿tiene usted algo así?** *(tee-en-ah oo-sted al-goh ah-see?)* which means "Have you got one like that?"

buenos días
bwen-nos dee-as
good morning

The rest of the book will show you many of the words and phrases you can use to make your stay in Spain even more enjoyable. Then you can go home feeling you know Spanish people a little better. You'll probably find they enjoy many of the same things you do.

Speaking Spanish is quite straightforward. Just make the sounds of all the letters in the word.

Meeting people

Spanish people have different ways of greeting people they meet. They use polite greetings if they do not know the person well. With close friends and family they are less formal.

Señor González meets someone he does not know well.

Buenos días, Señor Romero.
*Bweh-nos dee-as,
Say-nyor Roh-meh-roh.*
Good morning, Mr. Romero.

¿Cómo está usted?
Koh-mo es-tah oo-sted?
How are you?

Buenos días, Señor González.
*Bweh-nos dee-as,
Say-nyor Gon-tha-leth.*
Good morning, Mr. González.

**Muy bien,
gracias. ¿Y usted?**
*Mwee bee-en,
grah-thee-as. Ee oo-sted*
Very well, thank you.
And you?

Miguel and Carmen go shopping with their mother and meet some friends.

¡Hola! ¿Cómo estás, Carlos?
Oh-lah! Koh-mo es-tass, Kar-loss?
Hi! How are things, Carlos?

Muy bien. ¿Y tú?
Mwee bee-en. Ee too?
Fine, thanks. And you?

Adiós, Carmen.
Add-ee-os, Karr-men.
Bye-bye, Carmen.

Hasta luego, Julia.
Ass-tah lway-go, Hoo-lee-ah.
See you soon, Julia.

Señor González welcomes friends to his home for dinner.

Buenas tardes. Entrad, por favor.
Bweh-nahs tar-dess.
En-trahd, pohr fah-bohr.
Good evening. Please come in.

Buenas noches, mamá.
Bweh-nahs noh-chez, mah-mah.
Good night, Mommy.

Buenas noches,
Carmen. Que duermas bien.
Bweh-nahs noh-chez, Karr-men.
Kay dwair-mas bee-en.
Good night, Carmen. Sleep well.

Buenos días is used to greet people during the daytime, and **buenas tardes** in the afternoons and evenings. **Buenas noches** (good night) is used only at night.

When people meet, they often like to discuss the weather.

Buenos días, señora.
Hace calor hoy.
Bweh-nos dee-as, say-nyor-rah.
Ath-eh kal-ohr oy.
Good day, madam.
It's warm today.

Sí, hace mucho sol.
See, ath-eh moo-cho soll.
Yes, it's very sunny.

Making friends

The González family have gone to the beach and taken a picnic lunch. After lunch, Miguel and Carmen run off to play soccer on the hard sand while their parents sunbathe.

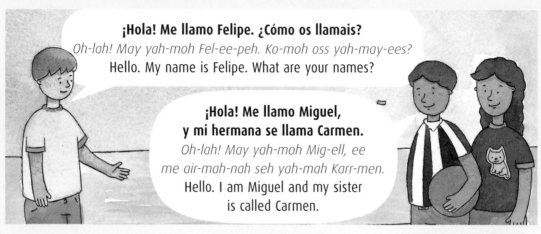

¡Hola! Me llamo Felipe. ¿Cómo os llamais?
Oh-lah! May yah-moh Fel-ee-peh. Ko-moh oss yah-may-ees?
Hello. My name is Felipe. What are your names?

¡Hola! Me llamo Miguel,
y mi hermana se llama Carmen.
*Oh-lah! May yah-moh Mig-ell, ee
me air-mah-nah seh yah-mah Karr-men.*
Hello. I am Miguel and my sister
is called Carmen.

Hola, Felipe.
¿Cuántos años tienes?
*Oh-lah, Feh-lee-peh.
Kwan-toss an-nyos tee-en-ehs?*
Hello, Felipe. How old are you?

Tengo diez años.
Ten-goh dee-eth an-nyos.
I am ten.

¿De dónde eres, Felipe?
Day don-deh air-ess, Feh-lee-peh?
Where are you from, Felipe?

Soy de Barcelona. Estamos de vacaciones aquí.
Soy deh Bar-the-low-nah. Ehs-tah-mohs deh va-kath-ee-own-es ah-kee.
I live in Barcelona. We are on vacation here.

Felipe introduces his friend from the United States.

The rest of the González family enjoys sitting in the sun.

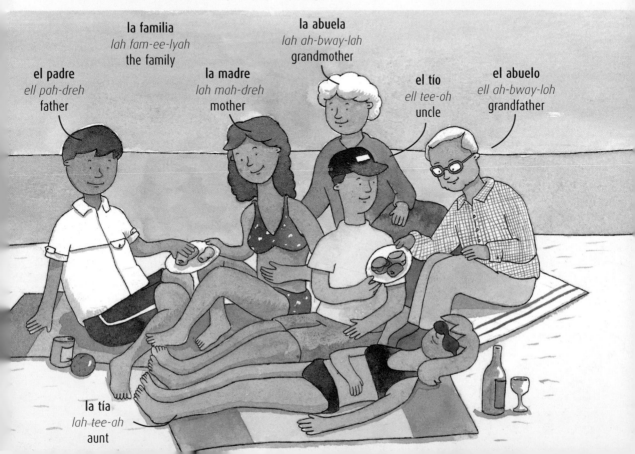

Finding the way

Miguel and Carmen go to the nearby town with their new friends, Felipe and Tom. They look for the park while their parents go shopping.

> **Perdone señor.**
> **¿Hay un parque por aquí cerca?**
> *Pair-don-eh sen-nyor.*
> *Eye oon par-keh por ah-kee thair-kah?*
> Excuse me sir.
> Is there a park near here?

> **Sí, está cerca.**
> **Está de tres minutes de aquí.**
> *See, ess-tah thair-kah. Ess-tah deh*
> *tress min-oo-toss deh ah-kee.*
> Yes. It's only three minutes from here.

> **Está al final de esta calle, a la derecha.**
> *Ess-tah al fee-nahl deh ess-tah*
> *ky-yay, ah lah der-reh-chah.*
> It's at the end of this street, on the right.

> **Gracias.**
> *Grah-thee-ass.*
> Thank you.

Helpful words and phrases for asking the way:

cerca de	junto de	enfrente de	delante de
thair-kah deh	*hoon-toh deh*	*en-fren-tay deh*	*deh-lan-teh deh*
near to	close to	opposite	in front of

44

 de nada *Day nah-dah* **don't mention it** ● **lejos de** *lay-hoss deh* **far from** ● **entre** *en-treh* **between**

On the way back to the square where their parents left them, the children get lost.

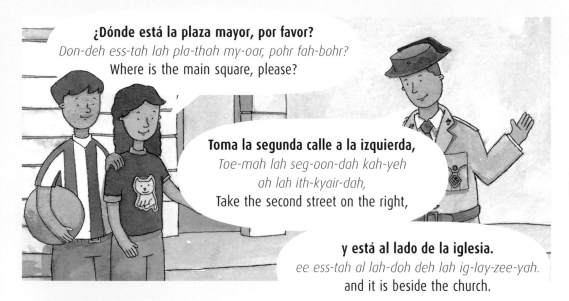

¿Dónde está la plaza mayor, por favor?
Don-deh ess-tah lah pla-thah my-oar, pohr fah-bohr?
Where is the main square, please?

Toma la segunda calle a la izquierda,
*Toe-mah lah seg-oon-dah kah-yeh
ah lah ith-kyair-dah,*
Take the second street on the right,

y está al lado de la iglesia.
ee ess-tah al lah-doh deh lah ig-lay-zee-yah.
and it is beside the church.

Useful places to ask for

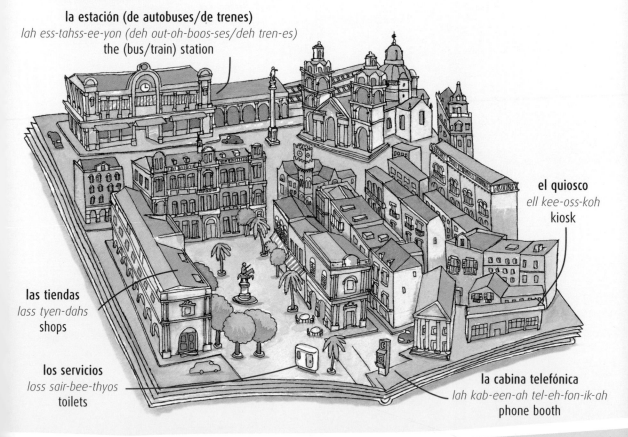

la estación (de autobuses/de trenes)
lah ess-tahss-ee-yon (deh out-oh-boos-ses/deh tren-es)
the (bus/train) station

el quiosco
ell kee-oss-koh
kiosk

las tiendas
lass tyen-dahs
shops

los servicios
loss sair-bee-thyos
toilets

la cabina telefónica
lah kab-een-ah tel-eh-fon-ik-ah
phone booth

junto de *hoon-toh deh* close to ● al lado de *al lah-doh deh* next to (or beside) ● detrás de *day-tras deh* behind

A visit to Barcelona

Felipe's parents have asked the Gonzálezes to visit them in Barcelona over the weekend. Miguel has been there once before, but Carmen has never seen Barcelona. They are staying in a hotel.

Hemos reservado dos habitaciónes en el nombre de González.
Ay-moss rez-air-bah-doh doss ab-it-ahth-ee-yohn-es en el nom-bray deh Gon-thah-lez.
We have reserved two rooms in the name of González.

Sí. Tienen ustedes las habitaciones números cinco y seis.
See. Tee-en-en oos-ted-ehs lass ab-it-ath-ee-yohn-es noo-mair-oss theen-koh ee says.
Yes. You have room numbers five and six.

Aquí tiene las llaves, señor.
Ah-kee tee-en-eh lass yah-bes, sen-nyor.
Here are your keys, sir.

¿A qué hora es el desayuno?
Ah keh or-ah ess ell deh-sah-yoo-noh?
At what time is breakfast?

Desde las siete, señora.
Dez-deh lass see-et-teh, say-nyor-ah.
From seven o'clock on, madam.

Miguel and Carmen are very excited. They can't wait to go and explore Barcelona with their parents.

Some of the sights of Barcelona

Casa Mila

Stadio de Camp Nou

Plaza de la Boqueria

Out and about in Barcelona

Not only is Barcelona the second city of Spain, it is also a center of business, fashion, the arts, and entertainment. The González family is going to meet Felipe's family at a café.

Quiero tomar el metro
Kee-air-roh toh-mar ell met-roh
I want to go on the subway

Yo también. ¡Por favor, papá!
Yo tam-be-en. Por fa-bor, pah-pah!
Me too. Please, Daddy!

They are waiting in the station for the train.

Dirección Cornella

¡El tren llega ahora!
Ell tren yeh-gah ah-oh-rah!
Here comes the train now!

Queremos la tercera parada.
Ker-reh-moss lah tair-ther-rah pah-rah-dah.
We want (to get out at) the third stop.

Before they set off to explore Barcelona, the two families choose what they want to drink at the café

Bueno, queremos dos cafés, dos tés, una limonada y tres coca colas, por favor.
Bweh-no, kair-reh-moss doss kaf-ehs, doss tehs, oo-nah lim-oh-nah-dah ee tress ko-kah ko-lahs, por fah-bor.
OK, we would like two coffees, two teas, a lemonade, and three Coca-Colas, please.

Muy bien, señor. ¿Quiere usted café solo o café con leche?
Mwee be-en, seh-nyor. Kee-eh-reh oo-sted kaf-eh so-loh oh kaf-eh kon letch-eh?
Certainly, sir. Do you want black coffee or coffee with milk?

Some places to visit in Barcelona

the real heart of the city

El Barri Gòtic

Barcelona's most famous street

Las Ramblas

49

Going shopping

Barcelona is a center of fashion, so Señora González wants to look at dresses and hats and perhaps some shoes.

Es muy atractivo, este vestido.
¿Dónde puedo probármelo?
Ess mwee ah-trak-tee-boh, ess-teh bess-tee-doh.
Don-deh pweh-doh pro-bahr-meh-loh?
This dress is very pretty.
Where can I try it on?

Los probadores
están enfrente, señora.
Loss pro-bah-dor-es es-tan
en-fren-teh, say-nyor-rah.
The changing rooms are
opposite, madam.

Miguel, Carmen, and their father want to go to the newsstand on the corner.
First, the children need to count their money to see what they've got!

¿Cuánto cuestan las postales?
Kwan-toh kwes-stahn lass pos-tah-les?
How much are the postcards?

Tres euros los chocolates.
Cada postal cuesta sesenta centavos.
Tres ew-rows loss chok-oh-lah-tes.
Kah-dah pos-tahl kwess-tah
say-sen-tah then-tah-bos.
Three euros for the chocolate.
Each card is sixty cents.

¿Y estas dos barras de chocolates?
Ee es-tahs dos bah-rass day chok-oh-lah-tes?
And these two chocolate bars?

There are good, colorful markets in Barcelona and in most Spanish towns and villages. These are some of the things you will see in them:

las lechugas
lass leh-choo-gas
lettuces

las naranjas
lass nah-rahn-has
oranges

las patatas
lass pat-tat-ahs
potatoes

las manzanas
lass man-than-nahs
apples

los limones
loss lee-moh-nes
lemons

los huevos
loss way-voss
eggs

Me gustaría comprar un periódico, por favor.
May goo-stah-ree-ah kom-prahr oon pair-ee-od-ik-oh, por fa-bohr.
I would like a newspaper, please.

Eating out

Soon, it will be time for the González family to leave Barcelona and return home. Before they go, they meet Felipe's parents for a meal in a restaurant. On the way, Felipe's friend Tom wants to mail his cards.

Me gustaría comprar cuatros sellos para postales a los Estados Unidos.
Meh goo-stah-ee-ah kom-prar kwah-tross say-yos pah-rah pos-tah-les ah loss Ess-tah-doss Oo-nee-doss.
I would like four stamps for postcards to the United States.

Son ocho euros, por favor.
Son otch-oh ew-rohs, por fa-bor.
That's eight euros, please.

Now that Tom has mailed his cards, they can all go to the restaurant.

¿Una mesa para ocho, por favor?
Oo-nah meh-sah par-rah otch-oh, por fah-bor?
Can we have a table for eight, please?

Sí, por supuesto. Venid ustedes conmigo, por favor.
See, por suh-pwes-toh. Bay-nid oo-sted-es kon-mee-goh, por fah-bor.
Yes, certainly. Please come with me.

In most restaurants you can choose a set menu for a fixed price.

¿Qué van a tomar?
Keh ban ah toe-mahr?
What would you like?

Tomaremos el menú del día.
Tom-ah-reh-moss ell men-noo del dee-ah.
We'll have the fixed menu.

Queremos pan, por favor.
Ker-reh-moss pan, por fah-bor.
We would like some bread, please.

¿Algo más?
Al-goh mass?
Would you like anything else?

Buen provecho, señores y señoras.
Bwen pro-beh-choh, seh-nyor-es ee seh-nyor-rahs.
Enjoy your meal, ladies and gentlemen.

53

A day out

The González family is back home again. Señor González is at work, but Miguel and Carmen are on vacation. Señora González takes them to the tourist information center to look for things to do.

Sí, señora, para niños el precio es media.
See, seh-nyor-rah, pah-rah nee-nyoss ell preth-yoh es meh-dyah.
Yes, madam, it is half-price for children.

¿Hay descuento para niños en el circo?
Eye des-kwen-toh pah-rah nee-nyoss en ell theer-koh?
Is there a discount for children at the circus?

Prefiero visitar el castillo.
Pref-yair-oh biz-it-ahr ell kass-tee-yoh.
I'd rather visit the castle.

No, yo quiero el cine. Adoro los dibujos animados.
No, yoh kyair-roh ell thee-neh. Ah-dor-roh loss dib-oo-hoss ah-nim-ah-doss.
No, I want to go to the movies. I love cartoons.

Vamos al castillo primero, y al cine por la tarde.
Bah-moss al kas-tee-yoh pree-mair-roh, ee al thee-neh por lah tar-deh.
Let's go to the castle first, and to the movies this evening.

54

 las cavernas *lass kav-air-nas* caves • **el estadio** *ell ess-tah-dee-oh* stadium • **el theatro** *ell teh-at-roh* theater

el helado *ell ell-ah-doh* ice cream ● el pirulí *ell pe-roo-lee* lollipop ● las palomitas *lass pal-oh-mee-tass* popcorn

Going to play

Carmen's school friend, Ana, wants her to go and play at her house. Her mother, Señora Ribero, phones Señora González.

Buenos días, señora González. ¿Cómo está usted?
Bway-noss dee-ass, seh-nyor-ah Gon-thah-lez. Koh-moh es-tah oo-sted?
Good morning, Mrs. González. How are you?

Buenos días, señora Ribero.
Muy bien, gracias. ¿Y usted?
Bway-noss dee-ass, seh-nyor-ah Ree-bair-oh.
Mwee be-en, grath-ee-ass. Ee oo-sted?
Good morning, Mrs. Ribero.
Very well, thank you. And you?

Ana querría invitar a Carmen
a jugar a nuestra casa. ¿Está de acuerdo?
Ana kair-ree-ah an-be-tah ah Karr-men ah hoo-gahr
ah nwes-trah kah-sah. Es-tah deh ah-kwair-doh?
Ana would like to invite Carmen to play at
our house. Is that all right?

Sí, por supuesto.
Carmen quisiera venir.
See, por suh-pwes-toh. Karr-men
kee-syair-ah beh-neer.
Yes, certainly. Carmen would
love to come.

56

¿Hacemos el concurso en la revista?
Ha-seh-moss ell con-coor-so enn lah rhe-vi-sta?
Shall we do the quiz in the magazine?

¡Ah, sí! Sería divertido.
Ah, see! Se-ree-ah dee-vairtee-doh.
Oh, yes! That will be fun!

**¿A qué hora tienes
que volver a tu casa, Carmen?**
*Ah keh or-ah tee-en-ehs keh
bol-bair ah too kah-sah, Karr-men?*
At what time must you be
home, Carmen?

**Dentro de una hora,
señora Ribero.**
*Den-tro deh oo-nah or-rah,
seh-nyor-rah Ree-bair-oh.*
In an hour's time,
Mrs. Ribero.

57

---

la mañana *lah man-yah-nah* morning • **la tarde** *lah tar-deh* afternoon/evening • **la noche** *lah notch-eh* night

Fiestas

Spain is a great country for fiestas, or fairs, and parades – colorful occasions that are full of life. Nearly all fiestas are held on saints' days or feast days of the church.

In many villages, towns, and cities, a statue of the local saint or the Virgin Mary is dressed in colorful robes and carried through the streets. In the evening, people eat outside and there is singing and dancing.

¡Mira! Por allí. La procesión viene.
Mee-rah! Por ay-yee. Lah pro-thes-syon bee-en-eh.
Look! Over there. The procession is coming.

Illness and accidents

Spain has good medical services. If something is wrong with you, you can usually be treated quickly and efficiently – although sometimes it depends which part of the country you are in.

Tengo dolor de cabeza.
Ten-goh do-lor deh kah-beh-thah.
I've got a headache.

Tienes que ir al médico.
Tee-en-ays keh ear al med-ee-koh.
You need to go to a doctor.

Here are a few little things that could go wrong.

Tengo dolor de estómago.
Ten-goh do-lor deh ess-toh-mah-goh.
I have a stomachache.

Se ha quemado.
seh ah ker-mah-doh.
She has burned herself.

Tengo fiebre.
Ten-goh fee-e-breh.
I have a fever.

Bits of me

If you have an accident and need the doctor, it's useful to know the Spanish words for parts of your body. And if you go shopping for clothes, here are the names of a few things you might want.

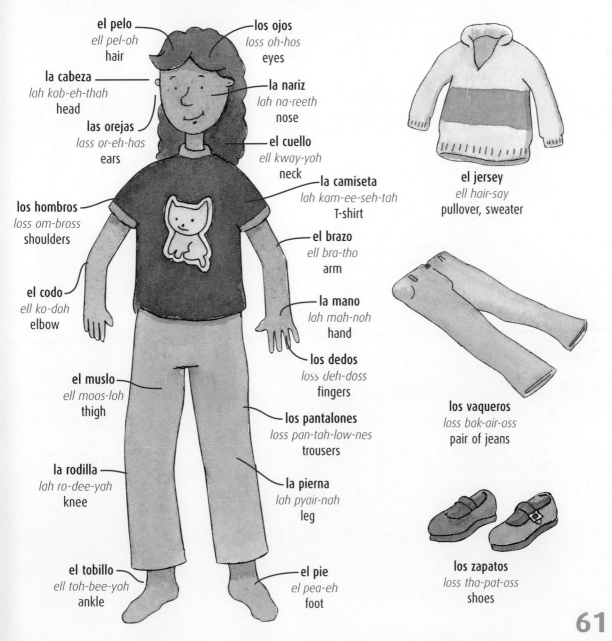

el pelo
ell pel-oh
hair

los ojos
loss oh-hos
eyes

la cabeza
lah kab-eh-thah
head

la nariz
lah na-reeth
nose

las orejas
lass or-eh-has
ears

el cuello
ell kway-yoh
neck

la camiseta
lah kam-ee-seh-tah
T-shirt

los hombros
loss om-bross
shoulders

el brazo
ell bra-tho
arm

la mano
lah mah-noh
hand

el codo
ell ko-doh
elbow

los dedos
loss deh-doss
fingers

el muslo
ell moos-loh
thigh

los pantalones
loss pan-tah-low-nes
trousers

la rodilla
lah ro-dee-yah
knee

la pierna
lah pyair-nah
leg

el tobillo
ell toh-bee-yoh
ankle

el pie
el pea-eh
foot

el jersey
ell hair-say
pullover, sweater

los vaqueros
loss bak-air-oss
pair of jeans

los zapatos
loss tha-pat-oss
shoes

61

la barbilla *lah bar-bee-yah* chin • **el estómago** *ell es-toh-mah-goh* tummy • **la falda** *lah fal-dah* skirt

Counting

1 **uno, una** *oo-no, oo-nah*

2 **dos** *doss*

3 **tres** *tres*

4 **cuatro** *kwat-roh*

5 **cinco** *thin-koh*

6 **seis** *say-is*

7 **siete** *see-et-eh*

8 **ocho** *otch-oh*

9 **nueve** *nway-veh*

10 **diez** *de-eth*

11 **once** *on-theh*

12 **doce** *dow-theh*

13 **trece** *treth-eh*

14 **catorce** *kat-or-theh*

15 **quince** *kin-theh*

16 **dieciséis** *dee-ay-the-say-ees*

17 **diecisiete** *dee-ay-the-see-et-eh*

18 **dieciocho** *dee-ay-the-otch-oh*

19 **diecinueve** *dee-ay-the-nway-veh*

20 **veinte** *bay-in-teh*

21 **veintiuno** *bay-in-tee-oo-noh*

30 **treinta** *tryn-tah*

40 **cuarenta** *kwar-en-tah*

1,000 **mil** • *meel*

50 **cincuenta** *thin-kwen-tah*

60 **sesenta** *sess-en-tah*

70 **setenta** *set-en-tah*

2,000 **dos mil** • *doss meel*

80 **ochenta** *otch-en-tah*

90 **noventa** *no-ben-tah*

99 **noventa y nueve** *no-ben-tah ee nway-veh*

100 **ciento** *the-en-toh*

100,000 **cientomil** • *the-en-toh-meel*

1,000,000 **un millón** • *oon mee-yon*

62

primero *pree-mair-oh* first • **segundo** *seh-gun-doh* second • **tercero** *tair-thair-oh* third

Telling the time

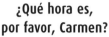

¿Qué hora es, por favor, Carmen?
Kay or-rah ess, por fah-bor, Karr-men?
What's the time, please, Carmen?

Son las cinco en punto.
Son lass thin-koh en poon-toh.
It's exactly five o'clock.

Son las once menos veinte
Son lass on-theh men-oss bay-in-teh
It's twenty minutes to eleven.

Son las once menos cuarto
Son lass on-theh men-oss kwar-toh
It's a quarter to eleven

Es la una
Ess lah oo-nah
It's one o'clock

Lo siento. Estoy de retraso.
Loh see-en-toh. Ess-toy deh reh-trah-soh.
I'm sorry. I'm late.

Son las once y cuarto
Son lass on-theh ee kwar-toh
It's a quarter past eleven

Son las once
Son lass on-theh
It's eleven o'clock

Son las once y diez
Son lass on-theh ee dee-eth
It's ten past eleven

Son las once y media
Son lass on-theh ee may-dee-ah
It's half past eleven

Es mediodía
Ess meh-dee-oh-dee-ah
It's midday (noon)
or
Es medianoche
Ess meh-dee-ah-notch-eh
It's midnight

63

In Spanish, one o'clock is singular, so they say **la una**, but all the other hours are plural.

Days, months and seasons

The Spanish do not use capital letters to start days of the week, months or seasons.

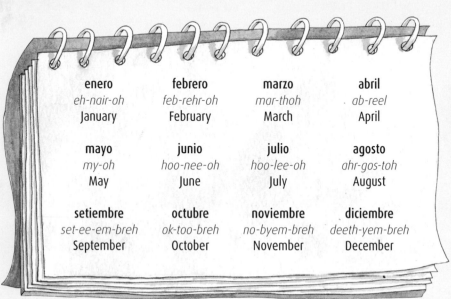

enero *eh-nair-oh* January	**febrero** *feb-rehr-oh* February	**marzo** *mar-thoh* March	**abril** *ab-reel* April
mayo *my-oh* May	**junio** *hoo-nee-oh* June	**julio** *hoo-lee-oh* July	**agosto** *ahr-gos-toh* August
setiembre *set-ee-em-breh* September	**octubre** *ok-too-breh* October	**noviembre** *no-byem-breh* November	**diciembre** *deeth-yem-breh* December

lunes
loo-nes
Monday

martes
mar-tes
Tuesday

miércoles
mee-air-kol-es
Wednesday

jueves
hway-bes
Thursday

viernes
bee-air-nes
Friday

sábado
sah-bah-doh
Saturday

domingo
doh-meen-goh
Sunday

Acknowledgments

© Copyright 2006 by **Tony Potter Publishing Ltd.**, West Sussex, England First edition for the United States and Canada published in 2006 by **Barron's Educational Series, Inc.**

No part of this book may be reproduced in any form, by photostat, microfilm, xerography or any other means, or incorporated into any information retrieval system, electronic or mechanical, without the written permission of the copyright owner.

All inquiries should be addressed to:
Barron's Educational Series, Inc.
250 Wireless Boulevard
Hauppauge, NY 11788
http://www.barronseduc.com

Written by **Duncan Crosbie**
Designed by **Trevor Cook** at HDA, Brighton and **Kevin Knight**
Illustrated by **Tim Hutchinson**
Edited by **Claudia Bloch** and **Sheila Mortimer**
Language consultancy by **Claudia Bloch**

ISBN-13: 978-0-7641-5955-8
ISBN-10: 0-7641-5955-0
Library of Congress Control Number 2005931816

Printed in China

9 8 7 6 5 4 3 2 1

☞ **Día del Trabajo** *Dee-ah del Tra-ba-ho* May Day (May 1st) • **Navidad** *Nah-bee-dad* Christmas